W0017894

USA-1000

Crab Orchard Series in Poetry
Open Competition Award

11-28-15

USA-1000

Sass Brown

POEMS BY SASS BROWN

Crab Orchard Review &
Southern Illinois University Press • Carbondale

Copyright © 2015 by Susan Brown
All rights reserved
Printed in the United States of America

18 17 16 15   4 3 2 1

The Crab Orchard Series in Poetry is a joint publishing venture of
Southern Illinois University Press and *Crab Orchard Review*. This series has
been made possible by the generous support of the Office of the President
of Southern Illinois University and the Office of the Vice Chancellor for
Academic Affairs and Provost at Southern Illinois University Carbondale.

Editor of the Crab Orchard Series in Poetry: Jon Tribble
Judge for the 2014 Open Competition Award: Adrienne Su

Cover illustration: *Thirsty Art*, by Lisa Schumaier; photograph by Joanne
Rojcewicz

Library of Congress Cataloging-in-Publication Data
Brown, Sass, 1971–
[Poems. Selections]
USA-1000 / Sass Brown.
    pages cm — (Crab Orchard series in poetry)
Summary: "This volume of poetry gives readers a bold and irreverent look
at childhood, family, love, and loss through an examination of everyday
things"— Provided by publisher.
ISBN 978-0-8093-3446-9 (paperback)
ISBN 0-8093-3446-1 (paperback)
ISBN 978-0-8093-3447-6 (e-book)
I. Title.
PS3602.R722855A6 2015
811'.6—dc23   2015014952

Printed on recycled paper. ♻

The paper used in this publication meets the minimum requirements of
American National Standard for Information Sciences—Permanence of
Paper for Printed Library Materials, ANSI Z39.48-1992. ∞

For my parents

And for Jamie, my everything bagel

CONTENTS

Acknowledgments ix

The Death of the Oscar Mayer Wiener Girl 1

ONE

Discarded 5

American Grooves 6

What I Learned from Television Medical Dramas 8

Peep Show 9

Letting Him In 13

Mixed Loads 15

TWO

At the Eye Clinic 21

First Word 23

Archaeopteryx 25

Hallmark Card 27

Stealing Casino 29

If My Name Were Michael 30

First Kiss 32

Practicing 34

THREE

Fortunate 39

Moving Sale 41

Bridge of Flowers: Shelburne Falls, MA 43

Insulation 45

Stumbling Love 47

No Tableau 49

Disappearing Act 50

FOUR

IF YOU'RE LOOKING FOR A SIGN FROM GOD 53

Like Love 54

A Response to the Critique of Subjectivity 55

Layaway Heart 56

Letter to the Better Business Bureau 59

Under the Kitchen Sink: A Found Poem 61

Simmer 62

Provides 100% Recommended Daily Allowance of Vitamins
and Minerals 64

Ball of Fire 65

FIVE

Moriarty, Allison: pp. 2, 18, 34, 35, 48, 50. 69

Cycling 70

He Wants to Take Your Picture 72

News from Home 73

Frieze 75

Dreamcatcher 76

The Inkwell 78

Wildcat Canyon 80

Notes 83

ACKNOWLEDGMENTS

The following poems in *USA-1000* first appeared in these publications, sometimes in slightly different versions and under the name Susan Brown:

The American Literary Review: "Peep Show"

Black Warrior Review: "Dreamcatcher"

Born Magazine: "He Wants to Take Your Picture"

The Chariton Review: "Bridge of Flowers: Shelburne Falls, MA"; "Cycling"; "Fortunate"; "Layaway Heart"; "Provides 100% Recommended Daily Allowance of Vitamins and Minerals"; "Wildcat Canyon"

Crab Orchard Review: "No Tableau"

Crazyhorse: "The Death of the Oscar Mayer Wiener Girl"; "Letting Him In"

The Florida Review: "A Response to the Critique of Subjectivity"

Gulf Coast: "Ball of Fire"

Hawai'i Review: "At the Eye Clinic"; "First Word"

Hayden's Ferry Review: "Archaeopteryx"

The Long-Islander: "What I Learned from Television Medical Dramas"

National Poetry Competition Winners, 1997: "Under the Kitchen Sink: A Found Poem"

Poetry Northwest: "Mixed Loads"; "Moriarty, Allison: pp. 2, 18, 34, 35, 48, 50."

Potomac Review: "Discarded"

Sonora Review: "American Grooves"; "Insulation"

Twentieth Century, Number 26 (The Pig Iron Series): "If My Name Were Michael"; "Like Love"

The Writer's Eye: "Frieze"

I would like to express my gratitude to my insightful readers during various stages of this manuscript: Jamie Kowalski, Roger Mitchell, Paisley Rekdal, Maura Stanton, Jon Tribble, and David Wojahn.

Thanks to the Indiana University MFA program for being such a warm, welcoming place to write. Special thanks to the IU poetry class of 1997: Karen Carcia, Jamie D'Agostino, David Daniels, Van Khanna, and Scott Stubbs. I couldn't have hoped for a more talented, supportive, or hilarious group of friends and colleagues.

Thanks to Lisa Schumaier and Joanne Rojcewicz for your artistry and friendship.

Thanks to the Bread Loaf Writers' Conference and the Vermont Studio Center for the generous gifts of financial support, time, and community.

Thanks to Adrienne Su for selecting this manuscript, and to *Crab Orchard Review* and Southern Illinois University Press for giving it a home. Thanks to Lisa Fay Coutley for sharing this wonderful, overwhelming experience with me step by step.

And thanks to Greg Orr and the University of Virginia's Creative Writing Department and Young Writers Workshop for giving me such a great foundation.

USA-1000

THE DEATH OF THE OSCAR MAYER WIENER GIRL

From state to state I rode atop the burnished bun
and crouched in the hot dog shell where I sweltered
six years. Far from my hometown prom queen crown,
I lived in this uniform, polyester glazed with grease.
When I died, they buried me in a coffin lined with mustard.

ONE

DISCARDED

It isn't heaven—that place where all the lost things go.
It's more like a junkyard: heaps of broken glass on a flat

dirt landscape, the leftover pieces after "fixing" your car,
the camera from your last vacation, film still coiled inside,

embryonic. Or the roll discarded, its images blanched,
forgotten twice. It's like the IQ test problem they gave me

in the third grade: *if you lost your watch somewhere*
on the football field, what is the most efficient path to find it?

And my answer? That's lost too, though I could still hear
the ticking, hours after the test; it must have seemed

like a pulse. How easily wishful thinking can trick you.
In *The Fly*, when the scientist teleports his cat to nowhere,

her anxious yowl haunts the lab, but only for one scene.
Where did she go, the family asked? Her body shattered

like a TV image, never reassembled, she's part of the air;
inhaled, she's part of their blood. I know what it is now—

that sound, bleating from somewhere inside, the heart's
endless call and no response: the drone of the missing world.

Every night between Flo's *Kiss my grits*
and the Brooklyn poetry of *Up your nose*
with a rubber hose, suburban families sang along
with the Jhoon Rhee Self-Defense jingle
and kids all across College Park begged for lessons.
One tied her black robe's sash around
her forehead, another leapt from the couch
to karate-chop the plastic flowered TV tray,
spilling peas like marbles on the carpet. Sure,
the ad was shoddy, probably shot in Rhee's
dank basement, his kids mugging it up
for the camera, but the song was catchy,
the phone number memorable. *Call*
USA-1000, Jhoon Rhee means might for right,
a girl lip-synched broken English, *Nobody*
bothers me, dukes clenched close to her chest,
and everyone listened:

                    a mother double-checked
the locks, slamming a hip against the door,
her neighbor scribbled Rhee's number
on the back of an envelope, even the dog
cocked a floppy ear to the speaker. No matter
that the Rhees' house sat next to a mini-mart
on the south side, the sign spelled *defence*
with a *c*; tykes and parents flocked
to their wood-paneled basement—wall-to-wall
straw mats, cabbage sizzling in soy sauce upstairs
where Mrs. Rhee handed each mother
a complimentary egg roll.

                  And then
they stopped coming, just like that. The Rhees
rented out their basement, watched neighborhood
kids skateboard in the street from their window.
On the other side of town, they imagined, parents
said, *Such a cheap hobby, and so close to home*,
doled out their measured affection: a hug
for a bruise, one kiss per cut. And the tears—
there were none. When suburbia discovered the article

Jhoon Rhee Killed in Mugging, parents tucked it away
somewhere safe, and all afternoon helped their kids
build a ramp in the driveway: the whole family filing
knots smooth, forgetting how wood wears each season,
wheels traveling in the same crooked grooves.

WHAT I LEARNED FROM TELEVISION MEDICAL DRAMAS

I started taping legs when I was two,
wire jutting out my dolls' bendable limbs.
Each afternoon, glued to the tube's fake truth,
I watched—everyone died in soft focus,
doctors detected disease from one cough
stuck like a bone in the throat. A troubled
forehead longed for a cool palm, a toe caught
in the bathtub spout loosened with soap. Label
your babies. Start each sentence with *I don't
know how to tell you this*. Healing's a trick
of white sheets and metal paddles rubbed flat
together, a jump-start to the chest. Quick,
doctor. I want you to test my flexed knees.
I need a sponge bath, stat. You're losing me.

PEEP SHOW

1. Doll's Doll

He woke me up. I was sleeping
and he woke me up for the scene:
a man licked whipped cream
off a woman's swelled breast,
a cherry dotting the nipple.
I knew my father just wanted
to show someone, my mother's back
turned away in their motel bed.
Even *she* was naked
at least once, though I still thought
I was my mother's miniature,
features abstracted like those Russian dolls
that fit inside each other, the smallest
with only a smudge for a mouth.
Home now, I catch my mother
flipping channels in the cable-dark.
Her eyes graze each body, flickering
from bed to bed, the woman's lashes
black as spiders' legs in close-up, lips
moving a half-second after her words.

2. Dirty Poem

A friend of mine takes off her clothes
at night for money so she has the day
free to write stories—the kind
I bought through mail order
in middle school, then highlighted
to pass to friends in class.
It's just a job, she says: four nights a week
she squats in her glass box,
men jacking off in front of her, pumping
quarters to keep the window open.

But here, at least, she's the main character—
she paints her toenails, she sucks a dildo
that glows in the dark, and all the while
mentally counting her tips
and mouthing what they ask to hear.
At least she's not the one who wipes
the booths down at closing.

If I worked at the Lusty Lady
I could make $100 for half an hour
but I'd have to change my name to something
provocative, though I know a stripper
named Candida and none of her clients
get the joke. They want a centerfold
with legs spread wide enough
for them to see inside. In my friend's fiction,
it's two women, one with eyes masked
by a bandana; the other, lips parted,
saying something like *love*.

3. Confessional

I've never been tied up. I've thought about it, though. *What did you
imagine?* I had this braided belt back in college that was always too big
for me. I imagined slipping it from the loops, wrapping the ends around
my wrists, then pinning him with my fists. *Who was he?* A lover I had
briefly, back in college. He liked to talk while we fucked—it wasn't *making
love*—sometimes about the size of his cock, which wasn't too impressive
so I always had to stifle a laugh. Other times he'd ask me what I wanted,
but I was too embarrassed to tell him. *Why were you embarrassed?* I don't
know. Maybe I was afraid my fantasies were too pedestrian for him. He
was a poet, so I was careful with clichés. Isn't that silly? I knew he'd be
into it. The idea was more arousing to me than actually doing it, I guess.
*That's easier for you, isn't it—dealing with your desires by making them
cerebral?* I don't think so. I mean, I'm hardly a prude. But I never had the
courage to try it. If *courage* is the right word. *What about your friend, the
one who dances at the club? Did you think she was brave?* I admired her,
sure. To get up there every night and become someone else; what woman
doesn't want to do that from time to time? Once I tried on one of her

costumes—this leather bustier with garters and five-inch spiked heels. I looked ridiculous. But what impressed me most was her attitude. She said that she felt empowered, even then, with men watching. *And you believed her?* Only partially. I can see her point, that she's not exploited if she's a willing participant. But I can't help wondering how much of that is just rationalization. Can desire ever be truly equal?

What about the movie you watched with your father? Did it appeal to you back then? Of course not. I remember laughing mostly because it was so silly—the whipped cream, the guy with his enormous dick—it was probably John Holmes, but of course I didn't know it at the time. *How old were you? Eight? A few years older? Did you know much about sex?* I knew the basics, maybe a little more. I'd seen my father's *Hustler* magazines. He kept them in a drawer by the bed, but they never were really hidden from me. Sometimes I was with my mother when she bought them. *Your mother bought them for him?* Sure. I never thought anything of it. *And now?* I don't know. It makes me sad that he needed them, even worse that she knew about it. It would be different if they read them together. Who knows—maybe they did. *And what about that night at the motel?* You have to remember that I was in a cot on the other side of the room. I probably begged him to let me watch. And it wasn't like he was getting off on it—he was laughing, just like me. It was like our own private joke. If anything, I loved him more for being frank with me. *But surely you recognize it now as a moment of questionable parenting.* Of course. I can't be sure how or even if it happened the way I remember. Just that I'm not ashamed to talk about it. That counts for something, doesn't it? *Where was your mother throughout all of this?* Hiding her face in her hands. *Seriously.* She was embarrassed by anything. If my father belched she'd act like she'd never heard anything like it. Like she'd never done it herself. Secretly, though, I think she thought it was pretty funny; she just wouldn't say so, like it was inappropriate. Of course her embarrassment only made me want to be just like him. *Who do you think you take after the most, your mother or father?* My father, I guess. But I'm not sure. Maybe my parents were more alike than I realized. It was my mother who told me about sex, after all; my father died right before I met my first boyfriend. How's that for a Freudian coincidence? And now my mother watches those late-night, straight-to-cable flicks by herself. What's that John Lennon tune? "Whatever Gets You Thru the Night." 'Salright. 'Salright.

4. The Good Parts

This morning I caught my neighbor naked
through open drapes, her apple-shaped ass
facing the window, leg slung over a man's hip.
Sure I lingered, and who wouldn't,
desire laid out before me like a diagram
in the medical text my parents kept
on the highest shelf, behind glass.
Even Barbie's nippleless breasts
seemed wrong to me back then,
so I pierced those plastic-molded scoops
with straight pins, made my androgynous
dolls into boys, a red ribbon dangling
improbably between their legs.

People are just paper dolls waiting
to be stripped down to their flimsy essence,
posed in constant want. But who says
they're not looking back at us?
What if the image in the glass
were a mirror, a microscope,
drawing each detail of our own lives
into focus? Past your gaze,
past the butt and tit and skin
a woman's breathing in that box.
She knows what you want, bound up
on the other side like a mummy
in a comic book, groping toward
the next frame. She is watching you.

LETTING HIM IN

Through the curtain's crack I can see him
toss his head outside, sweeping his hair back
into a makeshift ponytail. The day begins

when Gabe mounts his motorcycle
and my cat pads to the window, watching him rev
the engine five full minutes in the cold.

My dreams are like this: predictable stud
in black leather, leg jamming the pedal.
Some nights I hear a woman's voice

across the hall, her face rounding out
my peephole. I go to sleep early,
blanketed by desire. Ramona licks herself

in bed next to me, tongue-strokes smoothing
the same patch of fur ten times over.
Her ears perk even before the knock

and I stumble to unlatch the chain. Of course
Gabe's here to borrow something, barely
greets me before he scoops Ramona to his chest.

He looks mangy this close, smells less
like leather than a pillow's musky neck scent.
What if I pinned his hand to my breast?

Would it change the fact that he's here
for a toilet plunger? Before he leaves
I can't help it: I graze the small of his back

just enough to want all of him,
even his gritty stubble, his left leg
twitching like a dog's while he's waiting

by the door, in idle. My fingertips tingling
with touch, I imagine us pressing together,
his obvious strokes, or worse,

the oblivious *thanks for the plunger*, purposeful walk
back to his apartment. I can see him preening there,
tweezing the area between brows. And now

I've ruined it—the suspended sweetness of not touching.
I press my palm to his back again, pretend
I was just guiding him out. He gives me Ramona.

She will feel his hand on her coat for hours.
She will paw the band of light beneath the door.

Ululate. Imagine
my disappointment,
looking it up:

*to wail or lament
loudly.* My tongue
wants it to mean

something like waves,
a liquid jewel
for the mouth,

l's in cursive
hooking
other letters.

Loading laundry,
my dress assumes
the shape

of longing: ever-
shifting, like all forms,
in search

of a body. How
can the word mean
anything but promise,

its two *u*'s cupped
and waiting?
I empty the last

Cheer into the basket,
watch my mis-
matched socks'

intricate dance steps.
Mixed loads—
my panties

in your cuff,
your tee shirt clinging
to my slip;

lay me flat
to dry, then
reshape. I love

the whisk of denim
against silk,
the lush vocabulary

of fabric:
chambray, chamois,
chenille,

fragile words
to hand wash
separately.

Spots of dye
like lipstick prints
blot my dress:

trace affection,
subtle variations
of pink—

petal, thistle,
blush—a dozen
pastel shades

given shape
by naming them,
the way *green*

becomes *mist*
in catalogs,
a palpable vapor.

Ululate, undulate,
uvula. Who cares
for meaning

when sound
is everything,
the mouth so full

of desire,
converting color
into form?

Can't you see us
together,
trying on love's

bedazzling garments?

TWO

The intern's hand wobbles but he hits his mark:
one drop in my right eye and my pupil

is a wide umbra rimmed in a slim line
of blue. I lean into the chin rest

as he dims the light, sun to shade
in a wrist-flick. I can smell his hands'

sterile soap as he turns a knob
near my ear. *Your cornea*, he tells me,

points to a diagram on the wall with his pen light—
fundus, choroid—each curve and bump labeled,

parts of my own body I couldn't name before now.
Terms exotic enough to be serious, for a moment

I think I want the props of injury, a glass ball
smooth as a marble I could show off

like the dentures my grandfather clacked
to make me laugh, then dropped in the nightstand glass.

But even then, his eyes clouded with glaucoma,
I knew he was fragile; the tissue

dabbed at his eyes did its damage, fibers scratched
sharp as glass. Now the intern stains my eye

to see where the scratch glows deepest,
yellow as a crater in the dark.

When my father lay comatose,
my grandmother insisted I take a look:

his leaf-curled body, lids still as his mirrored
sunglass lenses. A week later she'd given up,

21

the machines still humming their tireless
breaths. Parts of him still worked,

she told me, his eyes might be gifts
for those who couldn't see; we should

give them away. But how could they look on strangers
with the same blue kindness? Eight years later

I scanned the tamped lumps of earth
next to my father's grave, my grandparents' heaven,

I imagined, a kind of perfect underground alignment,
murmuring their language of the dark.

At the most recent funeral, my grandfather's death
blotting out the last, the eclipse startled us,

bright and milky just moments before.
My cousin squinted through vent holes

in a baseball cap as the sky shut off
like a TV at night—nothing but silence

surrounding us, the isolated instants before sleep
when sight no longer matters.

FIRST WORD

What I said was *light*. How it must have felt
on my tongue, the clipped *t* in the long hall
of my open throat. Back then, anything I couldn't see

was monstrous; I only had words for *want*.
But now, call buttons depict my needs—
the stick-figure attendant, a fan, bulb—all within

a fingertip's reach. The train stitches
nearby towns with its silver thread, sutures
whole cities I've only traveled *through*.

Of course I'm seated in the back, crammed between
the constant flush of the toilet and strangers
announcing their lives to each other,

matter-of-fact: one trashes her husband
like she's on a talk show while he fetches dinner
from the café car, stoppers her baby's mouth

with a pacifier; another dabs her eyes, narrates
each accordion wallet photo, her daughter
chattering away in her lap, mostly nonsense,

syllable and sound, an occasional *Daddy*
when the mother mentions his name.
There's nothing they won't say. Twenty minutes

and already I long for silence. Lights stud
the sky: distant apartment windows of people
I could love, ticking through their days

without me. Even my neighbor drops off
in the seat next to mine, head bobbing
like one of those plastic birds dipping its beak

to water, then jerking back up. Overhead, the beam
cuts a circle on my jeans. Book abandoned
in my lap, I'm drowsy, word-stuffed but quiet.

I imagine my palm outstretched to the bedside bulb,
its glow enough, I think, to see everything.
If only that were true—if the future were just

the area defined by headlights, tracks stretching
indefinitely toward that place we think we want to be.
Why did I choose *light*? Why did I speak at all

that night when I could have cried? When did I learn
to cloak desire, each sentence polite, rational?
In a few hours the women will file out into the night,

their boundless speech puffing white and true
in winter dark. Till then their babies alternate between
babbling and screeching, compete with the brakes' whine,

wheel on steel. They can't know where they're headed,
toward which ordered cluster of syllables,
only that silence is a box they must tear through.

No wonder we're born crying, announcing
our fear to the world, no wonder we spend
our lives struggling back to that first word:

the amazement, the breath on the lips, the time
when light was still a fluttering open of blinds.

The desire announced itself
on wingbeats: arms extended,
fingers splayed, I closed my eyes
and leapt from the mound
of construction dirt next door.
I kept biology texts at bedside,
recited a litany of names,
birds I'd never seen
except in books. Detached,
I studied them beneath the glossy skin
of diagrams—these first birds,
before the feather, were just lizards
gliding low on flaps used as parachutes,
longing to lift from ground.

Each winter morning my mother
would feed the dull birds
I refused to watch
on our lawn, sparrows
spitting millet from their beaks,
bathing in puddles of dust
on the gravel road.
She rubbed suet into tree bark,
lined windowsills with seed,
studied them all season
as they smoothed oil
into slotted feathers
and rose on thermals
like the first birds we have
only fossils to imagine.

What they left behind
is more permanent than tracks,
preserved like the clutch of eggs
my mother found nestled
in onion grass. We kept them
for years in basement boxes
marked *Nature*: those shells,
a dried skate I found

at the beach, the crisp body
of a bee I pasted to cardboard,
dozens of feathers.
Sometimes when I'm home now
in my old bed, I can feel
a pulse swelling like a song
from the syrinx, calling
coot, woodcock, kestrel
calling in a language I thought
I'd forgotten or never understood:
nuthatch, nightjar, avocet, sparrow.

Smocked in red-and-white-striped polyester,
I started my first job exactly one year after
my father's death, unpacked ornaments

from their styrofoam wombs. A miniature train
chugged a circle in its clear globe, plugged
into a bulb socket; Baby's First Xmas frame,

heart-shaped cutout for a photo,
tinkled its endless rendition of "Santa Baby":
love, generic and plastic, about to be tagged.

And the cards, each with its own coded
display slot—who studied their printed,
perfectly genuine messages as much as the sender,

45 minutes and still trying them on:
You're the grandest, Dad! replete with the supplied
illustration? My father never cared for cards;

Christmas had to wait for his mug of coffee,
so I savored Santa's note, a full page beside
the last bite of sandwich. That first December

without him, I chose other people's gifts and sealed
mylar balloons, the pathetic, cheerful gas trapped
in bags. Ten minutes before closing, I cursed

those stragglers, the way their fingers glanced
over every row of figurines, swore they read
greeting card text like they awaited a next chapter.

Can I help you find something? I begged
the last woman, mittened hands still thumbing.
She addressed it right there at the counter, as if

you could sign up for sentiment like a class
at community college: drawing, maybe, a landscape
bristling with firs. That year Christmas was over

so fast. Bows and wrapping gathered for the trash
before noon. Still it seemed like hours waiting
for the water to boil that morning—and later,

Mom and I just stared at the blinking tree,
gifts stacked and back in their boxes,
our lives in front of us opened and immaculate.

STEALING CASINO

When my grandmother says, *this is the game*
in which we hate each other, it's just a joke,
I'm reminded by my mother's nervous laugh,
her vigorous shuffling. I sort quickly, lining up
the cards in their proper order—jack, queen,
king—laminated faces glancing away.

Every year since my father's death
we all lay fast, take what we need from each other.
That's the object, to swipe your opponent's stack
just when they're confident, before they take yours.
My grandmother's the expert. Widowed at 34,

she's practiced most of her life
for this moment, left to guard her daughter alone.
When you're learning, you get used to losing.
You've got to watch closely, my grandmother scolds
but my cards blur; I make the same mistakes.
That's what tradition means
in our family—only children, only daughters,

weakness repeating itself. What else
could my mother have done that fall, her husband
gone, no rules left to follow? *Strength is knowing*
when to accept help, she tells me,
though we both know it's the replacement
who has the power; the guarded have no voice.

How do you survive on nothing? My mother thinks
it's better to be the loser, to give away her highest cards
until it's really just my grandmother and me
playing, if that's the word for it, stacks amassed
and changing hands. *This is the way to win*,
she demonstrates, snatching all she can. Ultimately,
the game is hearts and clubs together,
twisted in strands like DNA and just as dire.

Because it was summer and afternoons set
on Big Wheels skidding into potholes
and the sting of mosquitoes dipped
into my neck, who cared where we'd be
in three months, glazed with September

and its clatter of facts, rising
cartoon-early for the trudge to the bus?
We set up our road-stand pitcher
of Kool-Aid—water and spit, a touch
of baby oil for flavor, magic markers

to tint the mixture purple. No one
was dumb enough to try it except Leslie,
Eddie's little sister. We were bad kids,
too clever for our own good. Even
as Mrs. Pickens fed her daughter ipecac

and we promised to stay apart, Eddie and I
kept fingers crossed behind our backs.
Summer's like that when you're young,
making you brave and curious. Later we played
in his backyard hammock, as usual: we'd face

each other, rocking hard until one of us fell.
But this time we ended up grass-stained, twisted
together. Eddie flushed and ran inside; I went home
and cried. When I told my father, he said
I was changing, but what did that mean?

I liked my life: dirty overalls and forts built
out of sticks, playing "Traffic Cop" in the driveway.
That was the summer my father taught me
how to be a lady: at restaurants, drag your spoon
slowly through soup, lifting it away,

then toward your lips to blow, gently, until it cools.
You have to cross your legs. At my age
he'd hid six weeks in my grandparents' shed,
fumbling the pucker his neighbor's blouse made
between buttons, while his teacher called out

his full name, daily, to an empty desk.
So what if he was discovered, smoke
from Parliaments fogging the shed's windows?
He was a boy and got what he wanted—
boarding school in Stockbridge, freedom

breezing through the streets. All I ever got
were Tinkerbell grooming kits, pierced ears,
and a powder blue two-wheeler I stowed
in the garage while Eddie's dirt bike
with matching black handle-streamers tore up

our dirt road, spitting gravel in its wake.
That fall, junior high divided us into Shop
and Chorus, and I dreamed I was Michael,
the name my parents had chosen if I'd been a boy.
Who would I have been—my father

in old photos, lying on his dorm room cot,
or Eddie next door in Pre-Algebra, stuffing
crumpled paper down the back of Amy's jumper?
Surely not this person in the mirror: features
indistinct and looming, the strange face of adulthood.

In the bathroom Jake and I lunged
at each other, my best friend timing us
outside the door, and all afternoon
my stomach whirled at each starched plaid shirt,
the smell of soap, a freckled upper lip.
Last week romance was exquisite mystery
whispered in someone else's ear,
but in that half-second puckered brush
I forgot where I was, my vision of what
this kiss could mean: someone to meet
in the hall between classes, a reason
to stroke on strawberry lip gloss.

We never spoke again; he started seeing
my best friend that summer at the pool.
She moved fast, had held hands
with three boys before him,
and knew the art of note folding.
Junior high was full of endless longing,
lockers opened on suave glossy pinups
with lips I memorized in practice.
Who thought I could love any harder?
The months that followed added
new names to my diary list,
all those hours spent pressed against
the back wall of some boy's closet,
between stacks on the school library floor,
just learning each other's mouths.

And each one I remember as I can—
Sean, who insisted we both kiss
a towel instead of each other, Eric
hiding in the upper berth of his bunk—
the boys who suddenly were all tongue,
all hand, one who asked me first,
who trembled, who reeked of his father's
aftershave, those with hard-ons hidden
in their jeans, one who kissed me
at the playground, in the backseat

while his mother drove me home,
on my child-bed, and those who knew
by some miracle of intuition
that the best kiss hovers open-mouthed,
almost doesn't happen at all.

I'm not as funny as the TV, not as patient
as their dog whose lip-flap they grip
and twist into grins. I don't know
which room belongs to which doll, where to find
Lizzie's special cup. I'm the nanny
so I don't play properly. When they pounce
on their parents' bed, I can only see the danger:
stray sheets tangled around an ankle,
a tumble to the bare floor. Still they teeter
on the headboard, masters of their playground
until Sadie slips and I scoop her into my arms,
murmuring, *you'll be fine, you'll be fine,*
to myself as much as her. Of course she's
not broken; risk has no real consequence
to her yet. She'll do it again tomorrow.

It's Sadie's bedtime—the usual haggling
over toothpaste and glasses of water.
But tonight she won't let me leave;
outside there are storms that tear the roofs
from houses, she tells me, and did I know
that people still live beneath volcanoes
even though lava can rain down
like fire? As a child, my own list of fears
began indoors: gym class and Pin Elimination,
where boys would peg my legs with a ball
to topple the bowling pin guarded behind me.
Even then I didn't really play, just froze
and let them go about the cruel business of games.

For Lizzie there is no sleep for another hour;
the piano looms, a beast with keys
for teeth. She plunks out the first few
halting notes, start and stop, too high
even for a child to sing along
though she does anyway, like air whining
out a prick-hole in a balloon. What will happen
next year when she performs

in the school pageant, Lizzie asks, unsheltered

by the walls of her practice room? For now
she plays on, scolds the clumsy steps
her fingers take; she needs to get it right.
It's a song we both don't know,
configuration of mysterious notes, yet
soon we're learning it together, a slow
minor key, already growing recognizable.

THREE

FORTUNATE

There's a place in Chinatown where we watch
a woman folding paper tongues into warm cookies,
edible origami. Imagine the contraption: wheel-shaped
oven with its tiny revolving waffle irons, and above,
the spouts which squirt out perfectly measured
dollops of saffron-colored batter. It takes moments
to bake on the bottom before the press falls, and one

by one they disappear into the oven to emerge
on the other side. Those that rotate more than once—
burned, misshapen—she spears and drops
fortuneless into a barrel. Others she plucks up,
selects a random slip from a paper pile, pats it
in the center of the cookie, and rests it on a moon-
dimpled tray to dry. The four of us watched

for almost an hour, until she shoved a bag
of damaged cookies into my hands, then nudged us
from the store. And so our quest resumed:
the best egg roll in DC, steaming and crispy
with just the right amount of grease. Still,
we always returned to the Magic Wok, mediocre
but comforting, and right across the street

from the two-bedroom I had shared with K.
for the past few years. Friends since high school,
we lived in a kind of blissful stasis,
moving trancelike through our days: shower, gym,
shower, work, couch. R. would pluck out
a random tune on the guitar, while P. and I debated
the relative merits of price versus portion size.

I saved all my fortunes that summer, placed them
behind the transparent-windowed driver's license
in my wallet, as if their magic could seep
into my standard police description:
*Eyes: blue; Hair: red; You have many things
to be thankful for.* But that's not fortune, just
an unappreciated statement of fact. We all longed

for predictions. I was 12 when I braved
Madame Tina's curtained back room studio,
but I nursed her words for years: I would marry at 27,
have two children, a boy and girl. No matter
that I never wanted kids, or that the four of us returned
for my 28th birthday, a whole new future depicted
on my palm. That night, we passed around the plate

of cookies in our favorite dive, cracking them open
with the deft touch of surgeons, afraid to damage
our delicate futures. *Should R. quit his job? Will my book
be published this year? When will P. get laid?*
The answers hardly mattered. We wouldn't have
believed them anyway. In six months, two of us
would be estranged; by year's end, two others

would move in together. K. always told me not to hope
too much for anything, and so I didn't, coming home
alone to a fridge filled with half-empty paper cartons:
Moo Shu; Kung Pao; Chow Fun—anything that sounded
exotic and foreign, remote as I was from myself.
How easy it was to simply exist. At night
sometimes, I walked by the burnished windows

of the Magic Wok long past closing, glimpsed
my darkened face in the pane. Loss is an old story,
and the only one who cares is the one who writes it.
We were friends; now we're not. As for the rest,
the future is uncertain business and it doesn't listen
to anyone, not even that woman in Chinatown, bent over
a conveyor belt of cookies that keep on coming.

From a block away we can tell
        this house with its sunken roof
                and yellowed grass is a lost cause,

but still you insist we stop. A woman sits
        behind her warped card table and offers us
                a shoebox full of jewelry. *Nothing but diamonds,*

she jokes, untangling greenish bracelets
        from adjustable gumball machine rings.
                No surprise, of course, but you can't resist

the challenge: one day last summer,
        you left a house like this with a gold
                and ruby brooch for 50 cents, but no

such luck today. *You have to get here*
        while they're setting up, you tell me,
                though an hour's difference at this house

wouldn't have mattered. At a community sale
        in Fairfax last week, others like us
                circled the neighborhood dozens of times,

waiting for the first glimpse of a figure
        behind gauzy curtains, the door's crack,
                and beyond that, who can say? Tables

of glassware a flashlight reveals
        to be crystal? Or rows of empty jelly jars?
                I'm not the only one with a good eye;

in the time it took to dash
        to the car for a dime, the vintage
                Land O' Lakes mug was gone. But here,

even a dime seems too much to ask
        as we scan the boxes' contents: half-used
                pads of paper, 8-track tapes, a dirty,

naked doll with one eye
        stuck shut. By then I notice
                the window, four small faces

pressed against its glass, so I stoop
        to take home something—a toy
                they've given up or outgrown, miniature

chunky versions of their parents'
        things: stove with a plastic T-bone steak,
                tool bench and ironing board in primary colors,

chore becoming play. For us, rising
        at half past five every Saturday morning,
                play becomes chore. Buy and sell,

want and discard, this lawn's a house
        with its insides out. *Everything must go,*
                the woman reminds us, then extends

a charm from her private stash—a tiny,
        silver baby's shoe. *My mother's,* she says,
                but for you I'll sell it cheap. We move next week.

She points up the road a bit, the house
        almost identical, chain-link fence
                hemming it in. Going home, we follow

the crude handwritten signs, their arrows pointing
        uncertain directions. We keep coming back
                to where we started—the houses all so similar,

the streets' generic names—until we watch
        for the kids waving from the window,
                their unaltered expressions, sure we'll find our way out.

I thought it would be *made*
of flowers. That is, after all,
what the name implies:
blossoming arch with vines
for girders, overwhelming smell
of jasmine. But there's just
this puny footbridge with plots

of dirt on either side
of the walkway, a few
scattered spates of tulips,
wire fence running its length—
the kind that borders
the playground in the projects.
Lately, everything disappoints me.

I'm still a tourist, just moved
a few months back,
so I believe the promises
postcards make, their colors
impossibly lush. I respect
the effort, the local women's club
on their knees and planting bulbs,

but why not call things what they are?
At best, this is the Bridge *with*
Flowers, and most of them dying.
I should have known when I saw
the sign on Main, two opposing arrows,
one for each of Shelburne Falls'
attractions—"Bridge Parking"

in one direction, "Potholes" the other.
I take things too literally, I know;
the Sugar House on Mohawk Trail
doesn't glisten like a freshly licked
snow cone, nothing worthy of *Hansel
and Gretel*. We hike the mountain
to find trees tapped for sap,

but it's too cold to see any drip,
not one amber morsel. We savor
the bits of maple candy
they dispense while we wait
on wooden benches—
two hours for breakfast. And so
I study the brochure's printed story:

the 40 gallons of raw sap
boiled down for a single gallon
of finished syrup, and the tiny
one-month window when it's good.
New home, new life—is that
what I expected? That Paradise Pond
would be Eden for me? If it ever was,

it isn't now; the sign reads
"No Swimming Any Season,"
all that promise buried under a crust
of ice, just to thaw untouched.
And yet without the wait,
the desolate, snow-coated months
of winter, how meaningful is spring?

For the locals, stirring steamy
vats of sap, it's harvest time,
and breakfast finally ready. Still,
how do they live all year for this:
these soggy pancakes, this barren pond,
this bridge of wood and steel?

INSULATION

Did I really think I could live
on Cream of Wheat and popcorn that winter,
dragging out of bed each day past noon?
Always a thick film between the world
and me; how distant I felt from myself,
like my hands reaching for the bathrobe

were just hands. All I knew of my neighbors
was their trash in the dumpster,
snow-muffled voices in the parking lot.
And the ones who came before, the lives
they left behind. Every now and then
they'd turn up in my room, bit by bit
in drawers, as a checkered dishrag,
a sock stuck behind the dresser,

lint. I watched my neighbors in windows
across the way, their gestures exaggerated
like pantomime—an embrace after breakfast,
an arm motioning *come here*. And me,
I felt like one of those fairground chickens encased
in my separate glass locker, performing mindless tricks:

rising to shower, lifting the spoon to my lips.
Dusk made me a hazy outline behind
the shades, insulation-gray and fading
like the past has for me now—I can't
even remember my old address, though
I must have mouthed it over and over

like a lozenge. Each morning, I seemed to leave behind
flakes of myself in the sheets. Lulled
by the faint, indecipherable song
coming from the next apartment, at night I became
a statue of want: stationary, touchless. I wonder now

if I could have pulled myself out of that season
I spent slogging underwater, why some nights
the music next door even seemed
to warm the walls with its beat
though I knew the rhythm was only temporary,
the walls still were doing their job:
holding in, holding apart.

STUMBLING LOVE

1.

During that window of day when we're awake
together, I imagine you across the ocean,
already edging into the next calendar square.
You say your apartment is almost all windows,
surrounded by beach on one side,
mountain on the other. On my side
of the world, I put my apartment to bed
and all night the light gleams on
in the living room, as if you're just rising
in there, slipping graded papers into
your pack. I'm sure there's a Main Street
where you are too; you will pedal its length
in my dreams. For now I try to wipe my mind
free of its dust, sweep it clean like
your emptied house, floor still speckled
with pennies, glinting copper stars.

2.

I'm too short to reach the ceiling;
even standing on the bed I can barely press
these glow-in-the-dark stars so they'll stick.
Later I sift through bills and flyers for your letter,
a fin sticking up in the metal cell. Bringing it
to my room is like letting everything in—
silkworms steaming on your plate, typhoon
spotting the page. At the grocery
I buy more fruit than I can eat; I pluck
the red leaf lettuce from its mist. Skimming
my fingers along the banister to my apartment,
your letter still hangs large in the air
like in that painting by Magritte, objects
grown to absurd proportions: the matchstick,
a tortoise shell comb, wineglass suspended
in front of cloudy walls. Since your letter
I want to touch everything, lie awake
all night to watch the stickers slip from the ceiling,
flakes drifting down. I wake each morning
a little drowsy, wrapped up in sky.

3.

It's a whim, this class I teach today
on love poems, an excuse to drone for an hour
about you, my heart flagging away.
I tell my students to think of specifics,
then quote Santayana—*the love of a thing
consists of the love of its perfections*—
though even that's not right. And yet,
your partly shaved cheek, the handwritten
step-by-step instructions for cooking rice, the way
you say *poem* as if it were a foreign word, twanging
po-eem. Maybe that's all we can hope for,
love concrete and flawed, sitting
stubbornly in the cupboard like vinegar.
Of course I have taught my class nothing
useful about love, just that it is a trick
of luck, a knot in the chest, a woman fumbling
around a cluttered apartment at night,
arms outstretched to the dark.

NO TABLEAU

I didn't drive you to the train
the day you left. Months before
we'd wake to its clang,
the rush of rails, and draw closer.
Time clicked by as in a theater:
suspended, a series of stills
we took for motion.

Now I stand on the platform, my bag
stuffed with brochures and trinkets,
waiting to board for home.
People with round-trips kiss
goodbye around me, and one by one
each window boxes a new face.

Even now, I hear you narrating:
*In 1896, the Lumière brothers screened
the first motion picture,* The Arrival
of a Train at La Ciotat, but these windows
aren't a filmstrip. There is no
persistence of vision to keep the past
printed on my eye. This is no tableau:
the train is leaving the station.

Outside, the bright burst of red
I know to be a neighbor's sweater
bobs steadily down the street
until it could be anything: arc
of an umbrella, finch's wing-flick,
even your latched satchel of papers.
From my window it's what I imagine
hope must look like: vague shape
in the distance.
                Some things
my mouth knows without asking.
So every gesture—sweeping stray hairs
from the tub drain, turning down
the bed—becomes a story
of departure. Indoors nothing grows
but residue, until I am a wispy figure
at the window,
                shed as husk.
You can live with the others now,
my garden of moss-covered icons,
as if my desire made you disappear.
What lasts is what leaves. I watch
the sky dissolve into dusk, the trees
lose their sheen. And the heart
clatters on: battered, bold, intractable.

FOUR

THIS IS IT. Every week I drive down Belle View Boulevard
past the Lutheran church on the corner, a new
prepackaged message of hope on their sign.
Where do they get those corny, modern-day proverbs?
GOD ANSWERS KNEE MAIL. I'm compelled
to write them down in a notebook I keep
in the glove compartment, a compendium of pat solutions
to faithlessness. Who is *my* God? The television,
with its endless voices to soothe me all night long?
The hunk of stale birthday cake I've been saving
in the back of the freezer for when I really need it?
Two years now, I've hauled myself to one lousy job
after another, cursing the slow drivers ahead of me.
ANGER IS JUST ONE LETTER AWAY FROM DANGER.
I was warned: you'll spend the first few years
after graduation subsisting on ramen noodles, a 25-cent
compressed meal stiff as a dry sponge. But such is the ego
of the writer, assuming the cliché can't be valid.
I bought a condo ten minutes from the house where I grew up,
five minutes from my high school, where each day
I promised myself: *soon*. TO HAVE MORE, WANT LESS.
As if it were possible to whittle desire down to nothing.
Isn't that what faith is—yearning for something far beyond
this world? What do I know about faith, daughter
of a Jew and Methodist, two nonbelievers
zippered together. I always felt sorry for my friends
who left the slumber party early Sunday morning, dragged
from snug sleeping bags at 7 a.m. by a dutiful mother.
Once I went with a girl to Easter service. I left with a clutch
of painted eggs and a coloring book with Jesus's placid face
on the cover. FREE TRIP TO HEAVEN: DETAILS INSIDE.
I'm sure the minister would be glad to have me: a young person,
he'd say, searching for meaning. As a writer, you're taught
to conceal craft; poems about writing are self-indulgent.
But for us, the only God is self, the one with the power to conjure
whole pages of text from nothing. There must be a handbook
to help him revise the signs, that man I never see
putting up a new message, while the Washington Monument rises
in the dark, a small white pencil in the distance.   53

On the TV there's so much
there's almost nothing:
an orgasmic woman lathers
in an airport bathroom,
overcome by botanical extracts,
someone's mixing batter
on channel nine that tastes
like love, and I'm just trying
to find the remote wedged
between cushions. It's not
the '50s, but tell that to
the woman snapping vacuum
attachments back into place.
Eureka Upright. So much needs
to be cleaned, and each thing
needs its own special tool.
Pledge Lotion. On my soap,
everyone's named after foliage.
Fern and Leaf argue the meaning
of a look, but it hardly matters;
she's already bedding Forrest
in the previews. Today Sponge.
All of my china has food patterns
on it, my drinking glasses
printed with miniature utensils.
Objects on top of objects, I like things
to be labeled with what they are.
Lorna Doone. If only people
were given brand names, I'd know
who to trust. Forget coupons!
I'd trade Vanish for Promise
without a thought. Who knew
there was so much to want,
or that naming
could make anything delicious,
until you forget how empty
the box is after you've sat in front
of the TV all day, lifting and lifting

such small comfort to your mouth.

These groceries, for instance.
The mail pursed between
my lips. I'm writing about my life
again. On the radio another
Whitney Houston ballad with love
in the title, voice heavy with generic
longing. I'm on the couch eating
my cereal dry, right out of the box.
I had to drag the clean sheet
flat along the floor to fold it;
I'm crocheting afghans
for men who don't sleep in my bed.
In England a woman played
"I Will Always Love You"
for six consecutive months.
Someone keeps hanging up
on my answering machine,
leaving me with computer advice:
If you'd like to make a call . . .
The cops had to break in
to shut off her stereo, still bleating
its pitiful anthem. I'm sick
of love's constant knocking
and no one there to answer.
The news condenses her to anecdote.
And what else is there
to report? Somewhere
there are fires, a baseball legend
has died, a shoot-out stalls
the 7-Eleven. See their hands
wrapped around billy clubs,
smashing the CD to silver
fragments: a note here, a word
there. I'm imagining her face
on the television, head cocked
to the stereo's green digital,
eyes glazed with repetition,
working the cord with her fingers.

The hastily
scrawled note affixed
to the plastic
hanger read *Hold
Susan Today.*
And there it hung

until closing;
the perfect dress—
gray embroidered
sheath with princess
seams cut on the
bias—vainly

awaiting my
return. Wasting
days that summer
at the mall, I
fondled products
at each pointless

specialty shop:
shower scrubs and
gels, beads, kitchen
gadgets, bulk bins
of organic
produce and spice.

I rarely bought,
just pulled the day's
obsession from
the rack, told the
sales girl to put
it on hold, and

it was mine for
an afternoon.
Sometimes it seemed
that things were all
I could count on.
Patiently, they

sat wherever
placed, waiting to
be useful: the
glazed ceramic
bowl for its splash
of milk; chenille

gloves yearning for
outstretched fingers
to give them shape.
What thing doesn't
want to be stroked
to life, to be

considered by
hands? A sweater
can mimic an
embrace, the way
the slub of silk
learns the body's

curves. How could I
know someone that
well, so close I'd
take on their scent,
their heat? Even
a mail-order

bride, acquired like
property, is
studied, tailored
to exacting
measurements. I
wish I *were* that

dress sometimes, all
silhouette and
shimmer, nothing
but surface, the
brilliant facade
we buy to wrap
our common lives.

This time it's my hair dryer. Sure,
there were warning signs—the smell
like burnt rice, the grinding like a pebble

stuck inside—but then to have it cut
off in mid-dry, and with the temperature outside
below zero again, how was I supposed

to go out last night and pretend everything
was okay? And that's not all. Last month
it was the bikini underwear, shrunk

in the delicate cycle, and me
left with this scrap of cloth the size
of a napkin. What can I do with that?

Of course, I could squeeze into them,
but you know how that is, stuck out
at a party or something, trying to back

into a corner and when no one's looking,
wiggling your hands into your pockets
to pull them up. What I'm saying is that

it's easier to stay in, not that I want to,
what with the phone's strangled ring
from dropping it too many times,

but at least I can turn the ringer off.
I can keep the drapes closed. You're right,
I do live alone, and maybe things mean more

to me than they should. It's not like
I'm one of those women with the plastic
slipcovers on the sofa. I use things.

And not that I mind the dark, but when
I reach for the light switch, I expect
something to happen. Who wants to go

to Kmart every other day for new bulbs?
Then I'd have to take a shower and clean
myself up, but what would I dry my hair with?

Sometimes I use the TV glow for light
and leave it on all the time. I like
the voices. They're not like real people,

the women on TV. They just keep talking
all day long and never expect a response.
But what if one day they suddenly stopped,

and all those little bits of image
dissolved to black and separated themselves
for good? What then? And, of course,

that's the point—how can I enjoy my shows
knowing that? You see, I used to be good
at taking things apart to see how

they ticked. I earned the Ms. Fix-It badge
in Girl Scouts, I had the hand that slapped
static right out of the radio, but that's

not important. What matters is my hair dryer,
just this cracked plastic shell, and the others,
in a landfill someplace where broken appliances go,

cords entangled and longing, still warm.
What doesn't want to plug in? I'm sending it to you.
Put it to your ear; hear the current's faint purr.

UNDER THE KITCHEN SINK: A FOUND POEM

Miracle-Gro, crock pot, acorn squash,
black currant nectar, sink stopper, skillet
with the Teflon peeling off, five kinds
of vinegar, trash. Do we need poems like this
in the world, even one-eighth of them
interested only in their thing-ness,
the feel of words on the tongue?
This poem goes nowhere. And now
it's too self-conscious, a skin without
a skeleton, an interest in surface.
There is no unspoken martini
in this poem, no hidden meaning, just love
for what stays long past its expiration
date. A poem should move
or make things move, should go beyond
the cabinet into the pipes
where water rushes through a clog
of orange rinds and coffee grounds.
Things go on existing without a glance.
Without vision, the nubby potato eye surveys
its surroundings and pushes out
toward the cabinet crack,
toward the useful, changing light.

1.

Something about the morning makes me
cautious. Stunned again by sleep's
amnesia, we're quiet, awkward
with each other. I wander your house
after you leave, searching for what might
give you to me: your wooden box stuffed
with crayons, cards tacked to the walls,
a stone turtle. Every love has its mythology,
I tell myself, artifacts in place of words.
By night we gush and release like a zipper
unbraiding its little metal teeth.
We can't help ourselves.

2.

Tonight I need no more than the fact
of hands and lips. I want to simmer
all afternoon like water just before
boiling, to skim the twisted roads
toward your house, a rug swept
along a hardwood floor. I want to stretch
like my fern toward any strain
of available light, desire and need
bound in an embrace. Let's trust
our bones: nothing but push and grow,
the sure click of unlocking each other.

3.

Today I wake and for a moment
surrender all ambition.
Your arm still crooked into mine,
sweet ache of coiling bare
into each other before the alarm
pulls us apart—only this,

not the coffee flakes we'll stir into water.
Not the early idle chat, agenda of separate days.
Today I think I'll hover on the rim
of sleep and wake a while.
Later, maybe, I'll write a love poem.

4.

This is to say thank you
for giving me back my elbow,
its dimples just right
for a tongue to nest.
Bone-bulb, one touch and suddenly
you're alive, you hinge, you flex
and bruise black as a socket.
That's why kissing your elbow
is best, because it's been forgotten,
an unappreciated knob. The body wants
what it wants. It bristles, it waits,
desire in a constant hum.

Who cares what's going on outside when we've got a six-pack
and squeeze cheese, 3.2 extra oz. free in the limited edition
commemorative can, and a flick on cable with less than
one star? If the remote were a Camaro, I'd be cruising
to glut on talk show smut. I'd give up my graduate degree
for an after-school special called *Forrest Hump* with a hunk
of beef in a G-string telling Sally Field where to put
her box of choc'lits. O God give every woman an EZ Mop shine,
cubic zirconia for her finger, and a handcrafted set
of mail-order knives for slicing, paring, dicing, mincing,
and much, much more! Make the room a soundproof booth,
our arms raised in *v*'s for reception. While next door
someone's translating *Beowulf* into ancient Sanskrit,
we'll be breaking into another box of Ho Hos
and toasting to layer after layer of chocolatey goodness,
swirling our tongues to find the delicious cream center.

Barbara Stanwyck as Sugarpuss, singing
"Drum Boogie" a cappella except for matchsticks
scratching their box in lieu of drums.
Past 2:00 Sunday morning, I wonder if it's true
that the average American will spend over a year
watching TV commercials. Earlier
this evening he smelled so warm, like bread
and soap grilled over a campfire, early fall.
I felt my bones twitch. Who knew I'd get lucky
flipping channels later, just in time
to see Stanwyck stand on two encyclopedias
to kiss Gary Cooper? My student said the poem
I gave her didn't make the hairs on the back
of her neck stand up, not even on the second reading.
Just once I want to come home to shelves of books
I've *read*, spines cracked and opened to the word
hands. I want the one lightbulb that never
burns out. At least my cat nips my calves
when I walk in, the last Goo Goo Cluster
still sits in the back of the fridge. Sugarpuss says,
Brother, that's corn, as if she'd read my students' poems
this week, the single tear always slipping down
someone's cheek in the last line. I tell them to forget
about neck hairs, just write about what's in the back
of the fridge. Why can't the Taster's Choice couple
stop talking about coffee and just percolate, already?
I think about the hammer propping up his window
all night, the moths throwing themselves
at the screen. Last week my grandmother sent me
an article from the *Post* about James Wright,
scribbled, *I had no idea poetry was getting so big*
on scrap paper, then, *How's your love life?*,
as if metaphor was the way to his heart, not just
a desperate linking of what is always, eventually,
separate. But I can't stop trying: when our elbows
brushed in the supermarket tonight, everything responded
as it could—the Pop-Tarts kept popping,

kernels exploded in their bags. Orville Redenbacher
would have been proud, the corn so full of longing
it strained to break out of itself like Wright's blessing:
blossom, blossom, and my heart still throbbing.

FIVE

It's strange to see someone you knew from high school in her underwear
everywhere. Black lace garters, body stocking, Wonderbra, what have
you. She's airbrush-flawless now, staring at me from this newspaper
circular, and of course I'm buying it: the artificial cleavage and her
bangs, I imagine, swept back by a cow's black tongue. She stands out,
here among the designer knockoffs; she's too good for discounts. Even
back in chemistry class, fully clothed, people watched when she'd bend
over the Bunsen burner. When Ms. Marcus left the room, Allie'd leave
her test tube for an eyelash curler and we'd steal to the storeroom where
I'd become her test case for the day, brown shadow smoothed across my
lids to make my blue eyes "pop." Of course, I can't be sure if that was
her, or just one of the endless Kellys that blur together in the yearbook,
a tribute to what really matters—the tilt of a head, lips freshly kissed
and re-glossed. What is it about beauty that stuns you, that made me
think I was more than her science project? In English class, she'd share
my textbook, answer every question while I read the lines over and over.
Maybe Keats was right, since under those layers—the foundation, blusher,
the sprinkle of powder—we're all stuck with the inequitable truth of
genes. And if someone else sees beyond that, past the ruddy skin and the
bump on the nose, beyond *is* to *might be*, what else does that make her but
beautiful? Still, it's hard to tell what's image among all these girdles and
undergarments with their secret panels, or who she is in harsh lighting,
a tag dangling from this nightie like a bookmark, reminder of who
knows what.

The man on TV asks, *Don't you want a tight
butt?* He's a study in spandex with the body
of a cartoon superhero, a work
of art with his own infomercial, a line of heart-
healthy products for just 50 cents a day
(results may vary), and with no

more to buy ever! I'm a smart woman: I know
it's a pitch, but my tights are getting *too* tight,
my diet always begins next Monday,
so this time I join a gym where my body
is a pair of human scissors on the skier, heart
throbbing with the shock of extra work

and no overtime, no pay for sweat but the work-
out itself. My trainer says I shouldn't worry; not
all progress is visible. Remember the heart,
a beefy muscle she'll help to make a tight
fist. It's crazy, really—all these bodies
crammed into a warehouse, laboring daily

on stairs that lead to themselves. On Sundays
I imagine God in spinning class, working
it. Who cares if he has no body?
Hazy vapor in the second row, notice
his perfect form, the mind-controlled pedaling, how tight
he is with the instructor. Take heart:

even God can't keep up sometimes, his heart
monitor beeping its shrill warning. Today
I'm light-headed and close
to collapse, working
hard to make less of myself. No
matter that I'm seeing food in every body

part: a thigh glistens like a ham hock. The body
needs fuel to function, something hearty,
not candy bars disguised as power. No
more mini-meals in sectioned trays or day-
long fasts; give me a burger with the works.
I'm tired of being uptight,

all body and no heart. I'm a processed work
in progress, stamped *Grade A* but past my date,
holding tight for the long ride to nowhere.

And why not? You're young and want
to be hung on his wall like the others,
wrapped in translucent pink chiffon.
You know what your mother would say:
He's not interested in your face.
But you could be his assistant one day,
fall in love over darkroom trays
of Dektol. So you agree to come
after business hours, even though
the room is empty when you arrive
and he asks you to wear his terry robe.

Backdropped in white, breasts bound by gauze,
you try to relax as he positions you,
ties scarves to a fan and dims the lights.
Only when he starts to rub your arms
do you see he's slipped his own shirt off.
He says you have talent,
later he'll shoot portraits for your mother.

These pictures lie. Their poses, your smile
in soft light, the hard fact of your nipples
are not proof, no more than his insistence:
It will feel good; you know you want to,
as if the logic of his hands was irrefutable.

A photo can take and be taken.
Though you leave before dark, before
he can slide a hand between your thighs,
you must have curled up later, alone
in your bed, as if you could make your body
disappear like the contact prints
you tucked behind your mirror.
You will keep them as documents, see them
instead of your reflection: captured,
permanent as the fear of being pried open.

In the practice room our clarinets
wailed their plaintive notes,
and Waynewood Elementary's
orchestra sighed a collective gasp
of wind. At the bell, Tracey and I
took our instruments apart, then chucked
their clumsy cases into the closet
and trudged to gym, sneakers in hand
and dangling from their laces
like weights. We knotted clover bracelets
in the outfield while Chester sat
benched again.

                If this were news,
the details would gleam precise
as the medic alert tags around
Chester's neck, but it's memory,
so I have to guess. This morning
I found the clippings my mother sent,
Tracey and Chester folded together
in the envelope. Seems like
he was always in the back of our
class photo, a secondary character
you'd have to read the novel twice
to catch. All kids are cruel
or cruelty's friends, so we rhymed his name
with the obvious. Of course we didn't know
what it meant, couldn't have imagined
Chester's dad fumbling drunk
into his son's bedroom.

                Even now,
the facts smudging black as a bruise
in newsprint, I can't believe
the article's deadpan delivery:
  . . . shot his father twice
in the head while he slept.
And then a second headline—
Clarinetist Receives Fulbright.

Back home, my mother's the keeper
of history: when it was time
she gathered my toys for retirement,
Tickle-Bee and Walking Mickey shipped
to thrift stores. Who knows
whose hands they slipped into,
what second life they might have.
I sometimes wish I were like them,
grown up twice, passed along like
a secret.
                    You see, we all started together—
how many times we must have brushed
by each other in the halls or at lunch,
always going somewhere. I'd like to say
these clippings together in their envelope
are coincidence, or that it was chance
I quit clarinet the year Chester moved
to a special school, but fact makes everything
deceptively obvious: our class photo,
the three of us in different rows.
And who knows what fact is? Even now,
Tracey says, *But we'll see what happens*,
as if the future were typing
for her, prospects fading in newsprint.

FRIEZE

After the funeral, after the last
dusting in the fields, the widow
can finally get to work. All the guests
gone and spring arriving, what's left
is what will soon fade: snow patches
the yard like lint, and the leftovers—
casseroles and cold cuts, a tough rind
of bread—rot on the table, more things
that need tending. It's her job,
you see, to dispose of what remains,
to carry his things down to the basement.
The house is strange without him,
full of inscrutable gestures: her son
kicks a ball against the porch all day,
neighbors keep calling, the dog settles
in the bed's hollow, everyone with
his own particular sorrow.
                                        The widow
boxes his books, condolence notes,
bundles herself in her husband's clothes.
She needs a work shirt: chips flicked
from her chisel coat everything
in the basement, marble flecks white
as flurries. She runs her fingers
over the identical figures: a couple
and their son composed in stone, as if
she could craft a thing to last
past death. And what else could they
be staring into, eyes flat and wide
as coins? The heavens, all sky and light?
She will carve late each night for weeks,
grief taking shape, so deep in that season
it hardly matters what comes next.

It's catching the wrong ones, this twig curved
to a teardrop above my bed, sinew weaving
mesh at its center. Sleep loses
me in its muddled story: my hands
palm pockets of air, my father's face
slackens, features gone to water. I watched

him die ten years ago but my watch
still reads 6:15, the mouth-shaped curve
of blood still stains the carpet. Face
facts: the dream's loose weave
keeps me, fumbling his neck with my hand
for a pulse that stays lost

in that room dreams only know. Let me forget
the constant tick of his watch,
skimming each second with hands
whisker-thin, the strands of hair wound
around his brush bristles, weaving
a wispy spiderweb. My face

drawn taut like a mask, on the surface
sleep preserves me in its ambered gloss,
but inside I thrash like a fish in its netting.
When can I give up this deathwatch,
leave the sleeping pills bottled, all curve,
full moons nestled in a cotton trance? Hand

clenching pen, I trace his illegible signature
as if it were my own, letters effaced
with each stroke and curve,
merged—not lost—
like that improv medley of "Someone to Watch
Over Me," instruments blending

a new song. Let the web's sticky weave
catch me instead of these dreams, handed
down in the mystery of genes, watch
his profile rise in my own face's
architecture as I grow more intense, more lost.
Cradle me womblike, rocked by a curve

of woven rope. I can face
the cupping hands, the room, even his lost
watch, my wrist circled by the band's invisible curve.

It sat like all objects, waiting
for someone's hands. As a girl
I remember lifting its hinged lid,
the glass cup inside sterile
and inkless. Did anyone ever prop it
on their slanted school desk, black
dripping down its blue-ridged sides?
I hope my grandmother used it once,
dipped a nib into the liquid
while she drew her journal
from the rolltop desk, but it's gone
now, along with its story. All I know
is that it sat for years on my grandparents'
end table. In their house, everything
was tempting, touchable: too much china,
too many things to split or shatter.
How do you wear a stain in a house
like that, prints tingeing everything
you touch? When I think of her now
I see her hands—the silver band
with its pear-shaped diamond drops,
her tight-trimmed nails, holding a bag
of shells. She leans in to me,
brushing bangs from my forehead.
But not all marks are visible; downstairs
in her workroom, the whorls
on her fingertips darkened. Past the crate
of Vernors, the line of stiff clothes,
I can see the tools in her hands:
plier and pick, glue she'd have to scrub
from her hands with steel wool,
while upstairs the inkwell remained
on display, another beautiful, useless
ornament. The past isn't clean, not really;
it's messy like her crafts—her pencil holder
and its collage of glossy pictures,
a beaded matchbox speckled with glitter.
And if the inkwell no longer has a story,
I want to give it one, bring it downstairs

where it belongs. A thing wants
to be functional, wants to dribble ink
in random splatters. And me, I want
to break china plates, to rouse
the noiseless past from its drawer
of bones. I want hands in my hair.
I want to set the inkwell on my desk,
overflowing reminder of what's left:
shell and matchbox, glitter and word.

We've driven the ridge by the bay all morning,
each turn another IMAX theater
in surround, so lovely it's almost boring.
I've always been a lousy traveler; I prefer
the guidebooks' glib summaries,
every trip neatly packaged, tourists posed
at the exact moment of discovery. As a child

I spent vacations in the backseat
never looking up from my book.
Mountains were just distant lumps
of dirt, my parents constantly calling
for my rapt gaze. Even now I ruin it
by planning; so busy fiddling with the map,
I nearly miss the view. But you say, *Forget it*,
you know where you're going, and sure enough,

soon you're twirling barefoot in the foamy grass.
It likes growing here, you announce.
For the first time, I can imagine you
in your new apartment, your lawn fringed
and dew-tipped, standing at attention,
your body a thing about to happen.

So long I've heard your tired voice each day,
fingernails clicking your office keyboard.
We'd meet outside for lunch, then lay the Tupperware
in front of us—jelly bleeding through sandwich bread,
a wilted bowl of greens we called salad.
I never thought you'd leave home, streets
always calling the same names. There are places

not on any map, views brochures can't show you.
See these redwoods peel back their soft skins
in layers? Here fruit is smooth enough to rub
against your cheek. And you've already found the path
to the lake, blue coaster set at the canyon's bottom,
as if your whole life had come down to this.

I can see your windows open to the night,
I can smell lemons in your hair, while outside
tourist traffic makes its rhythmic push
past all the things we've seen today,
all the things I may never get to see.
There's nothing in this world
I don't want.

NOTES

"The Death of the Oscar Mayer Wiener Girl": This poem references Randall Jarrell's "The Death of the Ball Turret Gunner."

"American Grooves": Events in this poem were inspired by an urban legend, not fact.

"At the Eye Clinic": For Bernice Brown (1914–93), Larry Brown (1912–94), and Lonny Brown (1941–86).

"Fortunate": For Karen Rudolph.

"No Tableau": There is no absolute documentation that *The Arrival of a Train at La Ciotat* was on the program of the first ten short films ever to be screened publicly in 1896. The exact title also is in dispute.

"Under the Kitchen Sink: A Found Poem": With thanks to Mark Halliday.

"*Ball of Fire*": The last few lines reference James Wright's poem "A Blessing."

"Frieze": Based on the stone marker "Commemorative Stela of a Family," Eastern Roman Empire, circa A.D. 230, marble, from the Fralin Museum of Art's collection at the University of Virginia, Charlottesville.

"Dreamcatcher": According to Sioux legend, dreamcatchers were hung in lodges and tepees to assure peaceful sleep. The good dreams slip through the webbing and slide down to the sleeper, while bad ones become entangled.

"Wildcat Canyon": For Jenny White.

Other Books in the Crab Orchard Series in Poetry

Muse
Susan Aizenberg

Millennial Teeth
Dan Albergotti

Lizzie Borden in Love:
Poems in Women's Voices
Julianna Baggott

This Country of Mothers
Julianna Baggott

The Black Ocean
Brian Barker

The Sphere of Birds
Ciaran Berry

White Summer
Joelle Biele

Rookery
Traci Brimhall

In Search of the Great Dead
Richard Cecil

Twenty First Century Blues
Richard Cecil

Circle
Victoria Chang

Salt Moon
Noel Crook

Errata
Lisa Fay Coutley

Consolation Miracle
Chad Davidson

From the Fire Hills
Chad Davidson

The Last Predicta
Chad Davidson

Furious Lullaby
Oliver de la Paz

Names above Houses
Oliver de la Paz

The Star-Spangled Banner
Denise Duhamel

Smith Blue
Camille T. Dungy

Seam
Tarfia Faizullah

Beautiful Trouble
Amy Fleury

Sympathetic Magic
Amy Fleury

Soluble Fish
Mary Jo Firth Gillett

Pelican Tracks
Elton Glaser

Winter Amnesties
Elton Glaser

Strange Land
Todd Hearon

Always Danger
David Hernandez

Heavenly Bodies
Cynthia Huntington

Zion
TJ Jarrett

Red Clay Suite
Honorée Fanonne Jeffers

Fabulae
Joy Katz

Cinema Muto
Jesse Lee Kercheval

Train to Agra
Vandana Khanna

If No Moon
Moira Linehan

Incarnate Grace
Moira Linehan

For Dust Thou Art
Timothy Liu

Strange Valentine
A. Loudermilk

Dark Alphabet
Jennifer Maier

Lacemakers
Claire McQuerry

Tongue Lyre
Tyler Mills

Oblivio Gate
Sean Nevin

Holding Everything Down
William Notter

American Flamingo
Greg Pape

Crossroads and Unholy Water
Marilene Phipps

Birthmark
Jon Pineda

Threshold
Jennifer Richter

On the Cusp of a Dangerous Year
Lee Ann Roripaugh

Year of the Snake
Lee Ann Roripaugh

Misery Prefigured
J. Allyn Rosser

In the Absence of Clocks
Jacob Shores-Arguello

Glaciology
Jeffrey Skinner

Roam
Susan B. A. Somers-Willett

The Laughter of Adam and Eve
Jason Sommer

*Huang Po and the Dimensions
of Love*
Wally Swist

Persephone in America
Alison Townsend

Becoming Ebony
Patricia Jabbeh Wesley

Abide
Jake Adam York

A Murmuration of Starlings
Jake Adam York

Persons Unknown
Jake Adam York